Baby Dinosaurs

Titles in THE DINOSAUR LIBRARY Series

THE DINOSAUR LIBRARY

Baby Dinosaurs
Eggs, Nests, and Recent Discoveries

Thom Holmes and Laurie Holmes

Illustrated by Michael William Skrepnick

Series Advisor:
Dr. Peter Dodson
Professor of Veterinary Anatomy and Paleontology,
University of Pennsylvania
and
co-editor of *The Dinosauria*,
the leading reference used by dinosaur scientists

Enslow Publishers, Inc.

40 Industrial Road	PO Box 38
Box 398	Aldershot
Berkeley Heights, NJ 07922	Hants GU12 6BP
USA	UK

http://www.enslow.com

Library of Congress Cataloging-in-Publication Data

Holmes, Thom.
    Baby dinosaurs : eggs, nests, and recent discoveries / Thom Holmes
and Laurie Holmes ; illustrated by Michael William Skrepnick.
        p. cm. — (The dinosaur library)
    Summary: Describes how different kinds of dinosaurs hatched their young
from eggs and explains how scientists have studied fossilized eggs to learn about
these prehistoric creatures.
    Includes bibliographical references and index.
    ISBN 0-7660-2074-6
    1. Dinosaurs—Infancy—Juvenile literature. 2. Dinosaurs—Eggs—Juvenile
literature. [1. Dinosaurs. 2. Animals—Infancy. 3. Fossils.] I. Holmes, Laurie.
II. Skrepnick, Michael William, ill. III. Title. IV. Series: Holmes, Thom.
Dinosaur library.
    QE861.5.H637 2002
    567.9—dc21
                                                                    2002009756

Printed in the United States of America

10 9 8 7 6 5 4 3 2 1

To Our Readers: We have done our best to make sure all Internet Addresses in this book were
active and appropriate when we went to press. However, the author and the publisher have
no control over and assume no liability for the material available on those Internet sites or on
other Web sites they may link to. Any comments or suggestions can be sent by e-mail to
comments@enslow.com or to the address on the back cover.

Illustration Credits: Michael William Skrepnick. Illustrations on p. 61 after Patten, 1951;
p. 80 after Grigorescu, Seclaman, Norman, and Weishampel, 1990B; p. 78 after Kérourio,
1981; p. 74 after Beetschen, 1985.

Photo Credits: © Corel Corporation, p. 85; Courtesy of Sankar Chaterjee, pp. 66, 77; Wayne
Grady, p. 6 (Thom Holmes); Shaina Holmes, p. 6 (Laurie Holmes); Thom Holmes, pp. 39,
53, 58–59, 62, 65, 73, 76, 89; Thom Holmes, from the collection of the American Museum
of Natural History, p. 34; Image #410760, Photo by Shackelford, American Museum of
Natural History, p. 55; Image #410765, Photo by Shackelford, American Museum of Natural
History, pp. 8–9, 56; Neg./Transparency #5789, courtesy of the Library, American Museum
of Natural History, pp. 70–71, 81; Michael Tropea, p. 7; Rick Wicker, 1996, Denver
Museum of Natural History, pp. 26–27, 28.

Cover Illustration: Michael William Skrepnick

CONTENTS

ABOUT THE AUTHORS

Thom Holmes is a natural history writer specializing in dinosaur science. He has dug for dinosaurs with leading paleontologists in the United States and South America. He has collaborated with Dr. Peter Dodson on several dinosaur-related projects during the past fifteen years.

Laurie Holmes is a science writer and editor, as well as a reading specialist. It has been her privilege to associate with many of the world's leading dinosaur scientists and artists through her work with Thom. Originally a teacher, she maintains that she is still teaching by writing and editing books for young adults.

On a dig in Patagonia, Thom Holmes holds part of the skull bone of what is currently known as the largest meat-eating dinosaur ever.

Thom Holmes

Laurie Holmes

AUTHORS' NOTE

In writing *The Dinosaur Library*, we enjoyed sharing the knowledge that allows scientists to understand what dinosaurs and pterosaurs were really like. The series covers all the suborders of dinosaurs, from the meat-eating theropods, such as *Tyrannosaurus rex*, to the gigantic plant eaters. It also includes the pterosaurs, flying reptiles that lived during the same time as the dinosaurs. We hope you enjoy learning about these fascinating creatures that ruled the earth for 160 million years.

ABOUT THE ILLUSTRATOR

Michael William Skrepnick is an established paleo artist with a lifelong interest in dinosaurs. He has worked on newly described dinosaurs with a number of the world's leading paleontologists. His original artworks are found in a number of art collections and reproduced as museum murals, and in popular books, magazines, scientific journals, and television documentaries.  Michael lives and works in Alberta, Canada, close to some of the richest Upper Cretaceous dinosaur fossil localities in the world.

Paleo art is a field devoted to the reconstruction and life restoration of long extinct animals and their environments. Since we cannot observe dinosaurs (other than living birds) in nature, we may never truly know their habits, lifestyles, or the color of their skin. In addition, the fossil record provides only a fraction of the remains of a wide diversity of life on earth.

Many fairly complete skeletons of dinosaurs have been unearthed in recent history. Others are represented by as little as a fragment of a single fractured bone, an isolated tooth, or a footprint impressed in once-wet mud. It is still possible to create a reliable portrait of unique, previously unknown creatures, but the accuracy of the art depends on the following:

- The quality and amount of actual skeletal material of the specimen preserved
- Discussion and collaboration with a paleontologist familiar with the fossil material and locality from which it was excavated
- Observation and comparisons to the closest related living forms
- The technical abilities, skill, and disciplined vision of the artist

The resulting artwork can draw the viewer back in time into exotic worlds of the ancient.

Season of the Eggs

The female titanosaur was a late arrival to the nesting site. She had come from a distant place to join the herd that had gathered there for breeding season. Male and female adults and juveniles were living on a lush plain that spread out for many miles. They were milling about at the foot of a sloping rise that made up the nesting site. Having come from great distances, they stayed in this area for several months. Here, they mated, the females laid their eggs, and the herd waited for the eggs to hatch.

It was also a time to rest. They fed on the abundant vegetation. But it wouldn't last forever. Such a large gathering of plant-eating dinosaurs would eventually strip the area of most of its greenery. After the babies had hatched and were able to fend for themselves, the herd would migrate to another area, where food would be plentiful again.

The late-arriving female had mated late in the season. She would be one of the last to lay her eggs. Some of the eggs had been laid several months before and were already hatching. The remaining eggs rested in their bowl-like nests, warming in the sun. The warmth helped the embryos to incubate.

It was a beautiful day except for some threatening storm clouds in the distance.

The lone female approached the foot of the nesting ground, eyeing the vast area for a spot to lay her eggs. There were clutches of eggs for as far as she could see. Each nest was a small, shallow bowl in the dirt about 4 feet (1.2 meters) across. They were dug in the sandy earth. Most of the nests were about 10 feet (3 meters) apart. This was just enough space to allow the mothers to walk in and out of the area without accidentally trampling on the eggs. Once a mother laid her eggs, she left the nesting area and joined the herd on the plain below.

The nesting site itself had little room for vegetation, but a few trees and ferns had managed to survive the seasonal visits of the sauropods. Several streams meandered through the nesting site. When the babies hatched, they would have ferns to eat and fresh water to drink.

Such a large gathering of plant eaters naturally attracted predators. Several Aucasaurus roamed in plain sight in the out-skirts of the area. The titanosaurs found safety in their large body size and in the size of the herd. The aucasaurs were reluctant to risk attacking healthy adult titanosaurs and survived for the time being by picking off aging or dying members of the sauropod herd.

Pretty soon though, they would have many defenseless hatchlings to eat if they could get past the adult titanosaurs.

The lone mother looked over the nesting site for an open spot to lay her eggs. The area was packed with nests. Among the many thousands of eggs, she could see the early signs of commotion caused by the first hatchlings. The babies emerged into the world ready to walk and eat and get into trouble, as babies do. The mother became nervous at the scene, desperate to find a nesting spot. Her body told her that it was time to lay her eggs.

She carefully strode into the nesting area, walking the paths between the nests. Her eye spotted a vacant patch and she headed for it. The place was a dried streambed. She pawed at the earth with her front feet. The sandy bottom of the streambed was packed flat and hard. It was more difficult to make into a nest than the moist and muddy earth on the slope in the rest of the nesting area. But a determined titanosaur mother weighing several tons does not worry about such things. She dug in and quickly completed a well-formed nest. Turning around, she positioned herself over the nest and began laying her eggs. After a short time, the exhausted mother was finished, and twenty-five eggs crowded the little nest. She stood there, resting awhile.

Hatchlings were beginning to pop up in greater numbers. This caught the attention of the adult titanosaurs at the perimeter of the nesting site. There was a ripple of activity in the sauropod herd. Adults began to move, gathering near the edge of the nesting area. Although they could not safely walk among the babies, their presence around the site would help ward off any predators.

The activity of the hatching babies also caught the eye of an aucasaur. His instincts were to attack the nesting area and pick off the helpless hatchlings.

The titanosaurs were still gathering to form a protective barrier around the nesting site. The lone aucasaur found an opening in their line of defense—the dry streambed where the last mother had ventured to lay her eggs.

The aucasaur leaned forward and crept along. If he saw hatchlings in a nest, he simply lunged forward with his jaws open to snatch one up whole. The babies were small. It would take many of them to satisfy the hunger of the large meat eater.

The aucasaur stomped through the site, snatching up hatchlings on every side and squashing unhatched eggs underfoot. He was too busy to notice anything else.

The mother titanosaur was following the streambed to leave the nesting area. The sight of the marauding aucasaur frightened her. Being alone, her only instinct was to flee. The meat eater's back was turned as she began to pass him.

Suddenly realizing that the mother was there, the aucasaur turned with a snarl to face her. He wanted to attack but the mother was large. This moment of hesitation would prove to be his undoing.

Instinctively, the mother swung her heavy tail around to defend herself as she fled. She smacked the aucasaur across the face, crushing his cheek and shattering part of his jaw. She quickly trod away, back to the safety of the herd.

The aucasaur was stunned. Every movement of his face caused a stinging pain. He staggered along the streambed, leaving the nesting site, trying to find a safe place to recover. Several other titanosaurs had begun to stand guard over the area. They jostled the injured aucasaur with their tails and bodies as he escaped. He stumbled along the streambed until it reached the edge of a nearby lake. He rested there.

The course of life can sometimes be changed dramatically by unexpected but natural events. One such event occurred that day at the nesting site. The storm that had been forming in the distance soon reached the titanosaur nesting area. It was a monster of a storm. It rained in torrents rarely seen during the breeding season. The gentle streams overflowed and drove a deluge of mud and sand over much of the nesting area.

Many of the unhatched eggs were buried, killing the titanosaur embryos inside by cutting off their air. Hatchlings were washed away. When the storm was over, a large part of the nesting area was covered in a smooth layer of silt and mud. Thousands of dinosaur eggs were buried underneath.

The wounded aucasaur met his end that day as well. The once dry streambed swelled with the waters of the flash flood. Unable to fight the sudden rush of water, he drowned. His body was pushed into the lake, where it was buried by sediment.

The mother titanosaur and most of the herd survived. She left the once green and fruitful plain for another stop on the migratory path of the titanosaurs. She would return one day during another breeding season to mate. She and the other mothers would lay more eggs to continue the cycle of life.

Authors' Note—The preceding story is a work of fiction but is based on scientific evidence and ideas suggested by paleontologists. You will find explanations to support these ideas in the chapters that follow.

- Fossil dinosaur eggs: Chapter 5 (Dinosaur Eggs of Many Shapes and Sizes)

- Egg nests: Chapter 6 (Dinosaur Nests)

- Fossil dinosaur embryos: Chapter 7 (Whose Eggs Were They Anyway?)

- Patagonian titanosaur nesting sites: Chapter 3 (Family Life) and Chapter 7 (Whose Eggs Were They Anyway?)

- Parental behavior in dinosaurs: Chapter 3 (Family Life)

- *Aucasaurus*: Chapter 3 (Family Life)

CHAPTER 1

DINOSAURS WERE BABIES ONCE, TOO

When people think of dinosaurs, the first image that comes to mind is usually that of a monstrous giant. Long-necked plant eaters the size of houses. Horned dinosaurs as big as tanks. Ferocious meat eaters as big as school buses. Yet every one of these dinosaurs began life as a baby hatched from an egg.

The discovery of fossilized dinosaur nests and babies has revealed that even the largest of the large dinosaurs began life as tiny versions of their parents. Dinosaurs hatched from eggs, like their bird descendants and all known reptiles.

These facts raise many interesting questions. How big were dinosaur eggs? How were they protected during incubation? Did they look like their parents when they hatched? How did they protect themselves while young and small? Did the parents have a role in their survival? You will find the answers

An adult pachyrhinosaur and its baby

to these and other questions about dinosaur eggs, nests, and babies in these pages.

To begin, let's understand what dinosaurs were and how they differed from other animals.

Dinosaur Basics

Dinosaurs were a special kind of reptile that no longer exists today. Many people assume that all dinosaurs were gigantic, but many were less than 10 feet (3 meters) long. The average size of the 120 best known dinosaurs is about 22 feet (6.7 meters). This number reminds us that dinosaurs came in many shapes and sizes. Some were not much longer than a football player's shoe, and some grew to half the length of a football field.

Dinosaurs were part of the group of animals known as vertebrates—animals with backbones. The first vertebrates were fish, followed by amphibians, reptiles (leading to dinosaurs), and mammals and birds. Dinosaurs first walked the earth about 225 million years ago. The last of their kind became extinct 65 million years ago.

All dinosaurs are divided into two large groups based on the structure of their hip bones. The saurischian ("lizard-hipped") group is comprised of the two-legged meat-eating theropods; the four-legged, long-necked, plant-eating sauropods; and their sister group, the two-legged plant-eating

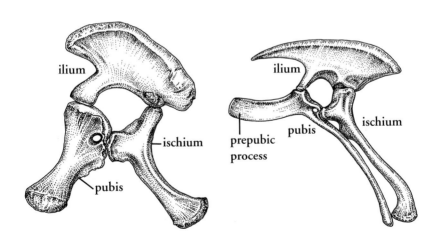

There are two kinds of dinosaur hips: saurischian ("lizard-hipped," left) and ornithiscian ("bird-hipped," right).

Table 1. Time Spans of the Dinosaurs

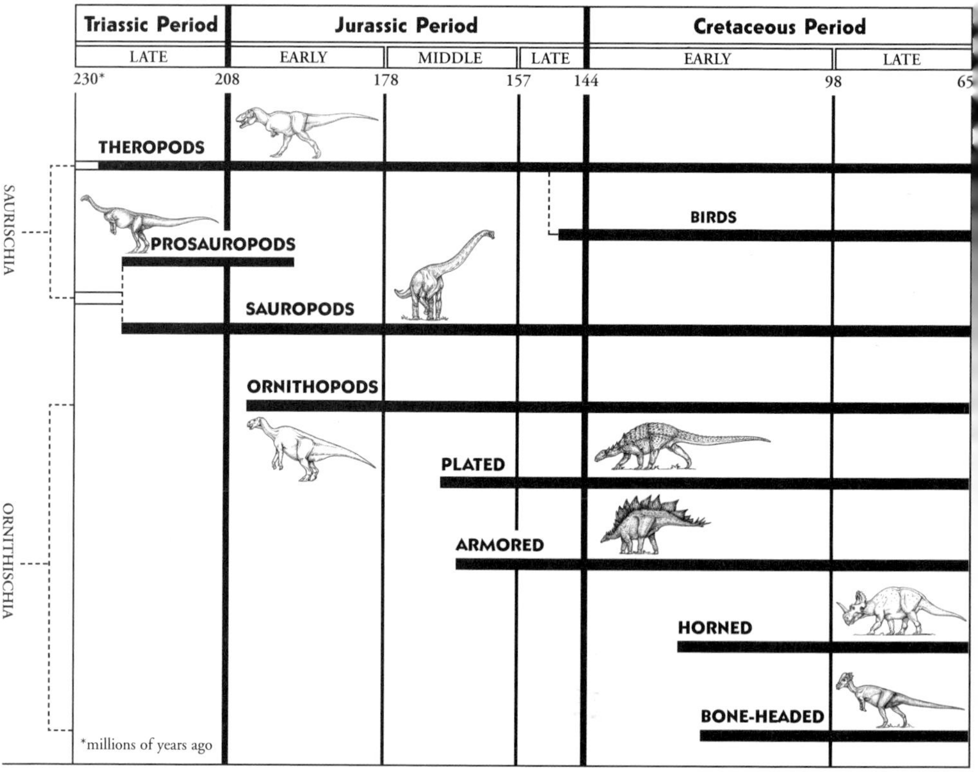

	Triassic Period	Jurassic Period			Cretaceous Period	
	LATE	EARLY	MIDDLE	LATE	EARLY	LATE
	230* 208	178	157	144	98	65

SAURISCHIA

- THEROPODS
- PROSAUROPODS
- SAUROPODS
- BIRDS

ORNITHISCHIA

- ORNITHOPODS
- PLATED
- ARMORED
- HORNED
- BONE-HEADED

*millions of years ago

prosauropods. The ornithischian ("bird-hipped") group includes all others, such as plated, armored, horned, duck-billed, and iguanodontid dinosaurs.

Both kinds of dinosaur hips allowed the hind legs to be attached underneath the body so that they could bear the entire weight of the dinosaur. This differs from modern reptiles, whose legs are attached to the sides of the body. A crocodile's legs, for example, cannot support its full weight except during short bursts of walking or running. The posture of the dinosaurs was stronger and more upright. In some ways, their posture was more like that of mammals than of other reptiles. Dinosaurs must have been more active and energetic than today's reptiles simply because it required more stamina to hold up their body weight. They were certainly far different from today's living reptiles.

Some dinosaurs were carnivores (they ate meat). Others were herbivores (they ate plants). Some dinosaurs walked on two legs, others on four legs. The major families of dinosaurs and when they lived are shown in Table 1. Most scientists agree that dinosaurs survive today in the form of birds. Otherwise, they all became extinct before or by the end of the Cretaceous Period.

Theropods ("beast-footed"). All of the meat-eating dinosaurs were theropods. They were the first dinosaurs to appear and among the last to become extinct during the 160-million-year reign of the dinosaurs. They evolved into several diverse kinds and sizes. All theropods walked

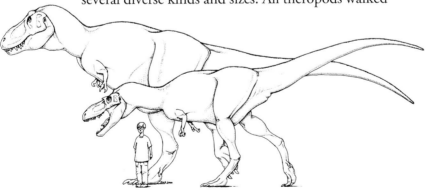

The enormous *Tyrannosaurus* towers over another meat-eating dinosaur, *Gorgosaurus*. They are shown in comparison with an average twelve year old.

on two legs, most had curved blade-like teeth for tearing flesh from their prey, and they were all equipped with special hand or foot

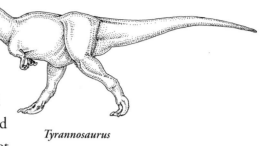

Tyrannosaurus

claws to help them catch and kill their victims. *Tyrannosaurus rex* ("tyrant lizard") is one of the best-known theropods.

Prosauropods ("before lizard-footed") and Sauropods ("lizard-footed"). Prosauropods and sauropods were long-necked browsing plant eaters. The most familiar sauropods, *Apatosaurus* ("deceptive lizard"), *Brachiosaurus* ("arm lizard"), *Seismosaurus* ("earth-shaker lizard"), *Diplodocus* ("double beam"), and others were the largest land creatures ever to walk the earth. The longest may have been about 150 feet (45 meters) long. The tallest could have looked over the top of a baseball stadium. The heaviest weighed between 90 and 100 tons. Prosauropods were the first of these two groups of dinosaurs to evolve. Even though they had large bodies, long necks, and small heads, they were not directly related to the sauropods that followed.

Brachiosaurus

Ornithopods ("bird-footed"). The ornithopods were a plentiful group of two-legged plant eaters that thrived for most of the age of dinosaurs. They filled a place in nature that is today occupied by cattle, moose, horses, antelope, and other peaceable plant eaters. Ornithopods

Heterodontosaurus

were the most successful and widespread of all herbivorous dinosaurs in the Cretaceous Period. They ranged in length from about 4 feet (1.2 meters) in *Heterodontosaurus* ("different-toothed lizard") to about 49 feet (14.9 meters) for the duck-billed dinosaur *Shantungosaurus* ("Shantung lizard").

Horned Dinosaurs. All horned dinosaurs are included in the order Ceratopsia. The name *Ceratopsia* means "horned face." It includes smaller, hornless varieties—such as *Psittacosaurus* ("parrot lizard") and *Protoceratops* ("first horned face")—as well as their

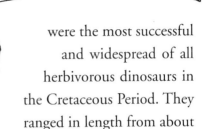

Protoceratops

famous horned cousins, including *Triceratops* ("three-horned face"), *Styracosaurus* ("spiked lizard"), *Torosaurus* ("piercing lizard"), and *Einiosaurus* ("buffalo lizard").

Ceratopsians were all herbivores. The largest of the horned dinosaurs were bigger than the rhinoceros. They thundered along on four legs and were decorated with exquisite horns and frills.

Styracosaurus

Stegosaurus

Plated Dinosaurs. The plated dinosaurs are also known as stegosaurs ("plated lizards"). The earliest stegosaur fossils were found in China and date from the Middle Jurassic Period, about 170 million years ago. They were 20 to 30 feet (6 to 9 meters) long. Familiar stegosaurs include *Stegosaurus* ("plated lizard") and *Kentrosaurus* ("spiked lizard"). The stegosaurs had large plates or spikes on their back and a set of spikes at the end of their tail.

Armored Dinosaurs. Armored dinosaurs are divided into two families, depending on whether they had a tail club or not. Those with clubs, such as *Euoplocephalus*, are of the family Ankylosauridae, and those without are from the family Nodosauridae.

They were 20 to 30 feet (6 to 9 meters) long. They all had extensive body armor in the form of bony plates.

Euoplocephalus

Armored dinosaurs date from the Middle Jurassic Period to the end of the Cretaceous Period.

Bone-Headed Dinosaurs. The bone-headed dinosaurs are from a family called Pachycephalosauridae. They existed during the Early and Late Cretaceous Periods. The pachycephalosaurs ("thick-headed lizards") had a thick, rounded cap on top of their skull that could be used to butt opponents. They were two-legged and measured up to 15 feet (4.6 meters) long.

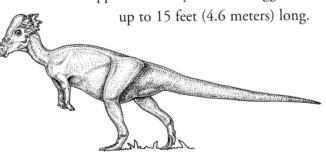

Pachycephalosaurus

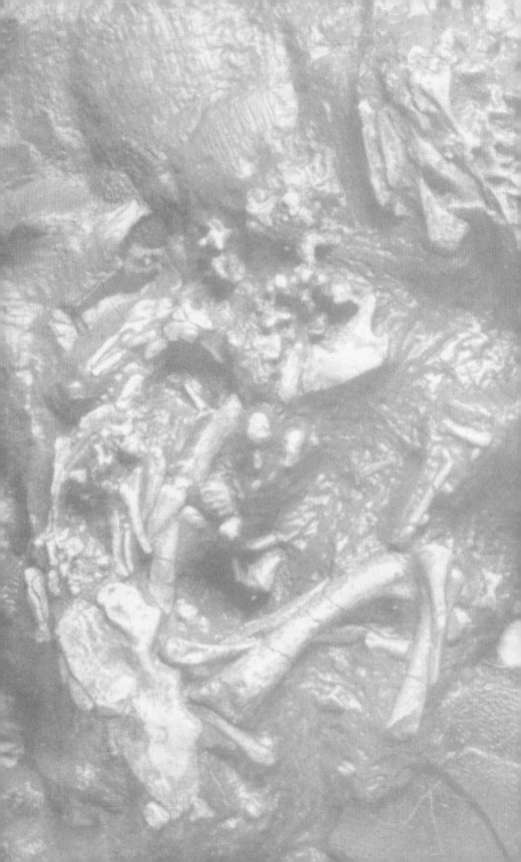

CHAPTER 2

DINOSAUR HATCHLINGS AND BABIES

All dinosaur babies had something in common with today's reptiles. From the moment they hatched, they had all the basic anatomical features of adult dinosaurs, except in miniature. They were probably able to walk shortly after birth, although feebly for a time. They were also able to eat the same foods as adults.

In contrast, many mammals and birds begin life in a helpless state. They are "babies" in that they require a period of growth and adjustment outside of the mother or egg to complete their transformation into self-sufficient organisms. These babies are often unable to see clearly, lack hair or feathers, are barely able to move, and require parental care for an extended period if they are to survive.

Although some baby dinosaurs may have received some care from their parents (see next chapter), all were ready to

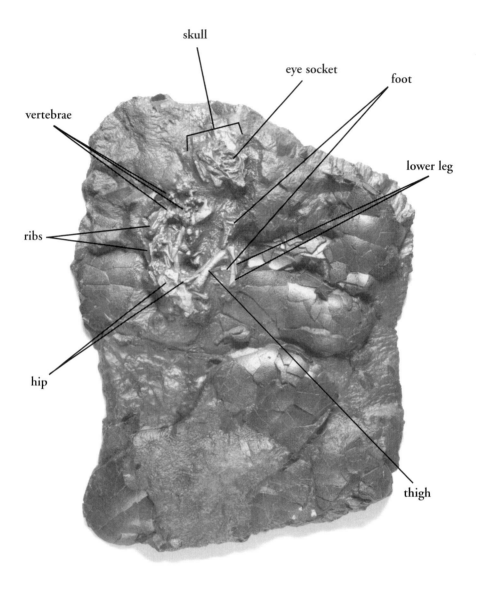

skull

eye socket

foot

vertebrae

lower leg

ribs

hip

thigh

This fossilized hatchling of a giant oviraptor (not named yet) was found on top of its clutch of eggs.

rumble into the world from the day they were hatched. What may have kept them in the nest under the watchful eye of their parents was their small size. Being tiny in the dinosaur world meant that there was a danger of being stepped on by a careless adult or being a target for someone else's dinner.

Discoveries of Baby Dinosaurs

Specimens of baby dinosaurs are unusual, but not as rare as those of fossil embryos. Good examples exist of newly hatched dinosaurs and other individuals at various stages of growth.

Sauropods were the largest animals ever to walk the earth. Yet their babies were tiny, barely as big as their mother's biggest toe claw. The jaw fragment of a newly hatched *Camarasaurus* indicates that the complete dinosaur was a mere 43 inches (109 centimeters) long when it hatched. Assuming that the *Camarasaurus* egg was round, it would have been about 9.4 inches (24 centimeters) in diameter.[1] An adult *Camarasaurus* was about 60 feet (18 meters) long—about 17 times longer than the hatchling.

The babies of another kind of sauropod, the titanosaurs, were even smaller. Specimens from South America were only about 15 inches (38 centimeters) long soon after hatching.[2] Although scientists do not know for sure, the adults may have been 40 to 50 feet (12 to 15 meters) long.

Baby sauropods grew to be about 15,000 to 20,000 times their original baby weight. If an eight-pound human baby grew that much, it would eventually weigh up to 160,000 pounds (80 tons).

A group of *Camarasaurus* travels along a shoreline. A baby *Camarasaurus* started out only as big as its mother's toe claw.

A baby *Apatosaurus* enjoys a meal.

Specimens of baby *Protoceratops,* a primitive horned dinosaur, were one of the highlights of the Mongolian expeditions of the 1920s made by the American Museum of Natural History. The discovery of a remarkable series of skeletons of this animal, from hatchling to adult, is one of the most complete growth series ever discovered for any kind of dinosaur. The smallest specimens, barely out of the egg, show a remarkable resemblance to their parents except for the frill on the back of their head. The smallest skulls were only about 4 inches (10 centimeters) long. The frill was but a ridge along the back of the neck until the dinosaur reached its "adolescent" years.

The even tinier skeletons of baby psittacosaurs went unnoticed for nearly sixty years in the storage rooms of the American Museum of Natural History. There they were left unstudied until paleontologist Walter Coombs, Jr., "rediscovered" them in 1982. Also from eastern Asia, these tiny skulls and partial skeletons represent *Psittacosaurus* hatchlings. The skulls measured only 1.1 to 1.7 inches (2.8 to 4.3 centimeters) long. The total body length of these babies was only about 10 to 16 inches (25 to 40 centimeters).

A *Protoceratops* mother brings food to its young.

The skeleton of a baby *Protoceratops* is on exhibit at the American Museum of Natural History in New York.

Little is known about the nests, eggs, and babies of the armored dinosaur family. It would be interesting to know how quickly an armored dinosaur developed its extensive armor plating. Were they born with armor or did it grow over time as the animal matured? A remarkable set of specimens of the Chinese ankylosaur *Pinacosaurus* ("board lizard") provides some answers to these questions. More than fifteen specimens have been found, ranging from juveniles to adults. Kenneth Carpenter has studied these dinosaurs to see how their armor plating and tail club developed as the animals grew. At about 5 feet (1.5 meters) long—a little less than half the size of an adult—*Pinacosaurus* showed the beginning growth of armor plating on its snout and neck, but no tail club was present. When the dinosaur grew a little more, to about 7.5 feet (2.3 meters) long, armor was present on most of the skull bones, some body armor was present, and the tail club began to grow. When it reached nearly adult size, at about 10 feet (3 meters) long, the skull and body were completely armored and the tail club had reached its full size.[3]

Another study of baby dinosaurs has been made by Jack Horner of the Museum of the Rockies at Montana State University. His work at Egg Mountain in Montana has revealed more about these creatures than just their size. Horner has pieced together clues from the environment of an entire hadrosaur nesting site to paint a detailed picture of duck-billed dinosaur family life. The story of *Maiasaura* and its young follows in the next chapter.

CHAPTER 3

FAMILY LIFE

Knowledge of the lifestyle and behavior of ornithopod dinosaurs has been greatly enriched by the discovery of their fossilized eggs, nests, and young. No other kind of dinosaur has told us more about how they lived and behaved than these two-legged plant eaters. This is mostly due to the pioneering work of paleontologist John "Jack" Horner. Since the late 1970s, Horner, together with his students and coworkers, has studied the stunning remains of eggs, nests, and skeletons found at many fossil sites in northwestern Montana.

We know from these discoveries that at least some kinds of ornithopods nested in colonies and took care of their young until they were able to leave the nest on their own. Many of these eggs and nests belonged to *Maiasaura* ("good mother lizard"), so named because of evidence that these duck-billed dinosaurs cared for their young. Their behavior is strikingly similar to that of modern birds.

From 1978 to 1983, Horner and his colleagues unearthed a bonanza of *Maiasaura* eggs and babies that date from about 80 million years ago (the Late Cretaceous Period). The team had discovered three nesting sites consisting of 14 nests, 42 eggs, and 31 babies.[1] Larger specimens of *Maiasaura* at various stages of growth were also found, although a good adult skeleton is still lacking. The discoveries were astounding in many ways. In only a few short years, Horner's team not only uncovered a new species of hadrosaur, but also succeeded in painting a colorful and astonishingly complete picture of the lifestyle, growth stages, behavior, and ecosystem of these gentle giants. It was perhaps the most revealing dinosaur discovery of the entire twentieth century.

The discovery of *Maiasaura*, its nests, and its babies began with a trip to a rock shop in the tiny Montana town of Choteau in 1978. It was there that Jack Horner and his friend Bob Makela were given a coffee can full of baby dinosaur bones. Marion Brandvold, the owner of the shop, later took the two paleontologists to the field site where the bones had been found, and the hunt for baby dinosaurs was under way. This first dig resulted in the discovery of a *Maiasaura* nest with the remains of fifteen 3-foot- (0.9-meter-) long baby duck-billed dinosaurs still inside. The work of a few days expanded steadily to cover a few years as the team continued to discover nests, eggs, and the remains of maiasaurs of different sizes.

The eggs were laid in bowl-shaped nests about 6.5 feet (2 meters) across and 2.5 feet (0.8 meter) deep. The mother *Maiasaura* may have dug out the nest in the mud with her hind feet, then mounded the rim with her forefeet and muzzle. The nest was then covered with vegetation such as pine needles to protect and incubate the eggs.[2] There could have been as many

The discovery of *Maiasaura* babies began at Marion Brandvold's rock shop in Montana.

as twenty eggs per nest.[3] Most puzzling was the fact that the eggs were always found in tiny fragments and with no obvious pattern to their arrangement. It was as if they had been trampled underfoot repeatedly for a long time, which is probably exactly what had happened. This became apparent when the scientists took a close look at the bones of the babies that were found in the nest.

The baby *Maiasaura* dinosaurs found in the nests were sometimes up to 3 feet (0.9 meter) long. Horner noted two intriguing features of the skeletons that have been interpreted different ways. The teeth of the young were well worn and the joints in their legs were weak, which would have made it difficult for them to move about. Horner interpreted these facts to mean the hatchlings were eating but not capable of

After eight or nine months, *Maiasaura* babies began exploring the world beyond their nest.

During the time the *Maiasaura* babies stayed in their nest, a parent dinosaur brought them food.

leaving the nest to fend for themselves. It became apparent to Horner that the *Maiasaura* babies remained in the nest for as long as eight or nine months.[4] If this were the case, then the young dinosaurs were defenseless and helpless while they were living in the nest. This could mean only one thing: There was an adult dinosaur looking over them, protecting them from predators, and bringing food to the nest for them to eat, the way birds care for their young. The reason the eggshells had been pulverized in the nests was that they had been stomped on for many months by a brood of active, nest-bound youngsters. His view of the evidence, and the picture forming of a large adult hadrosaur taking care of its nestlings, inspired Horner to name the dinosaur *Maiasaura*, meaning "good mother lizard."

Horner believes that the smallest of his *Maiasaura* specimens were actually unhatched embryos. This would explain their extremely small size and undeveloped leg joints. Horner's interpretation of the *Maiasaura* evidence is not accepted by all. Some scientists point to the worn teeth in Horner's *Maiasaura* "embryos" as evidence that they had already hatched. But even the evidence of worn teeth does not prove with certainty that the specimens were not embryos. Horner also discovered embryonic remains of another ornithopod, *Hypacrosaurus*, within an egg and they, too, showed tooth wear prior to being hatched.[5] He suggested that the dinosaurs were grinding their teeth prior to leaving the egg. Another group of scientists has found a case of embryonic tooth-grinding in a sauropod dinosaur, further reinforcing Horner's belief that his tiniest *Maiasaura* specimens were embryos.[6] Others have suggested that this discovery disproves Horner's picture of parental care.

Making Horner's portrait of hadrosaur family life even more fascinating is the fact that the nests themselves were part of a larger nesting ground. The nests were about 23 feet (7.0 meters) apart, which is about equal to the estimated average length of an adult *Maiasaura*.[7] This suggests that the dinosaurs nested together, in peace, and made room for an entire herd in a manner similar to that of colonizing birds today. Nesting in colonies made good sense for these dinosaurs. Because the young were helpless for many weeks, keeping them together in a nest protected them from predators and gave them time to grow until they could blend in with the herd. Except for an occasional raid by a small theropod such as *Troodon* ("wounding tooth"), a snake, or

another predator, a nesting ground with hundreds of nests and adult *Maiasaura* would have been a safe haven for the duck-billed dinosaurs living within its bounds.

Horner's team also found several deposits of nests and eggs in different layers of rock. This strongly suggested that the dinosaurs repeatedly returned to the same spot to lay their eggs. This led Horner to picture a large herd of migrating *Maiasaura*, perhaps 10,000 strong,[8] making their way back to the same nesting grounds year after year.[9]

The fate that doomed this nesting ground and its many inhabitants must have been swift and fierce. It was a fairly flat

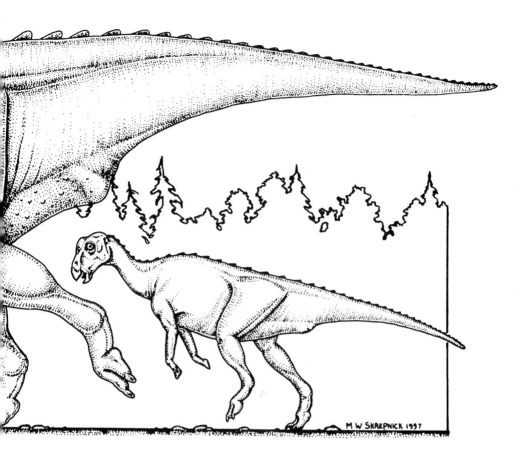

Fossils of *Hypacrosaurus* embryos have been found still inside their egg. The dinosaur is shown here with its young.

plain 80 million years ago, laced with streams connected to an inland sea about a hundred miles away. The area was probably flooded seasonally by torrential rains. Each year during the rainy season, after the breeding season was over, some of the leftover nests were probably covered with mud. But it wasn't a flood of water that sealed the fate of Horner's herd of nesting duckbills. They appear to have died from a massive volcanic eruption that rained hot ash and poisonous gases down on them. There they were laid to rest, covered with the smoky soot of volcanic cinder, entombed in the earth, doomed to become fossils that would one day reveal their most amazing story millions of years later.

Other Loving Parents

The picture of hadrosaur life painted by Horner is compelling and challenges us to understand a lively interpretation of fossil evidence. But he is not alone. In recent years, other evidence has come to light that helps scientists interpret the family life of dinosaurs.

While fossil hunting in the early 1920s, Roy Chapman Andrews discovered many dinosaur fossils in Asia. Among them was *Oviraptor* ("egg thief"). *Oviraptor* was a small meat eater. The position of the adult dinosaur, with its arms outstretched over its brood of eggs, leaves little doubt that this dinosaur was protecting its nest. It may have even been trying to shelter its eggs from the sandstorm or other natural catastrophe that was about to overcome them.

Another revealing fossil site in Mongolia clearly showed that other kinds of dinosaur hatchlings sometimes remained in the nest after being hatched. In 2000, David Weishampel of Johns Hopkins University reported on a *Protoceratops* nest that contained fifteen hatchlings. They had all perished in a sudden, catastrophic sandstorm. In death, the skeletons all faced the same direction, seemingly trying to gain shelter in a corner of the nest. There was no eggshell found in the nest.

This evidence suggests that the hatchlings were residents of the nest, probably in the care of an adult dinosaur that was not present when the catastrophe buried the babies alive.[10]

The Family Life of Sauropods

A vast titanosaur egg site in Patagonia, Argentina, also suggests that these dinosaurs had the same behavior as *Maiasaura*. In Patagonia, these dinosaurs occupied a large nesting ground but made just enough room for one another to make nests and lay their eggs. The nests were usually spaced about 9 or 10 feet (3 meters) apart. This made for cramped quarters in the nesting ground for the large, long-necked

A nesting oviraptorid protects its eggs.

plant eaters. Each mother laid between 15 and 34 eggs in a shallow pit formed in the mud. The adult titanosaurs left the immediate egg site after laying their eggs. Otherwise the mothers would have trampled the eggs and the site would have been littered with broken eggs and eggshell, which it is not. The remains of adult titanosaurs and trackways, or fossilized footprints, near the nesting ground show that the adults may have stayed close to the site after laying their eggs. But did they watch closely over their nests after the young had hatched, similar to Horner's duck-billed dinosaurs?

Luis Chiappe and Lowell Dingus, who led the Argentinean expedition, cannot say for sure. But they suggest that the adult titanosaurs may have stayed near the nest area for several months, protecting its perimeter from intruding meat eaters.[11] Two large predatory dinosaurs are known to have frequented the site, including the 20-foot- (6-meter-) long *Aucasaurus* ("Auca lizard"), a recently discovered dinosaur.[12] (*Auca* is from the place they were first discovered, near Auca Mahuida.) *Aucasaurus* was a dangerous theropod about half the size of a fully grown titanosaur. It probably roamed the perimeter of the adult titanosaur herd that gathered there, picking off weak members. This predator may have also ventured into the nesting area once the hatchlings began to appear. The young titanosaurs, barely over a foot (30 centimeters) long, would have been easy pickings for a large carnivore.

Scientists also concluded that the same nesting site had been used repeatedly, possibly for many successive breeding seasons. They discovered at least four layers of egg sites on

Hypothetical Aerial Map of Auca Mahuevo Nesting Site

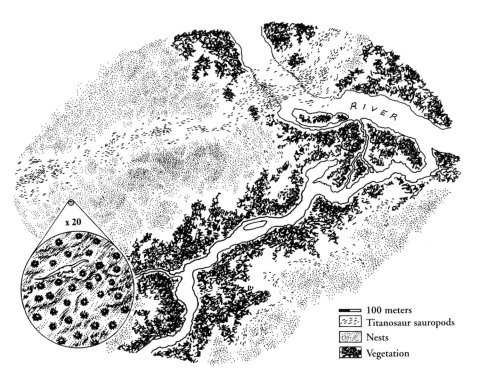

x 20

100 meters
Titanosaur sauropods
Nests
Vegetation

A look at a possible layout for the nesting site of Auca Mahuevo in Argentina shows just how many nests could have been present. Each dot is a nest; each slash is a sauropod. A magnified view of one small area shows how a sauropod may have walked between the nests.

different geologic levels, which means they were laid at separate times. A picture of the days of these dinosaurs was further completed by the discovery of fossil sauropod trackways near the site. These trackways confirmed their theory that the titanosaurs traveled in herds.

How long did the babies stay in the nest? Did the parents take care of them in any way? Chiappe and Dingus offer an intriguing idea about the life of the newly hatched titanosaurs. They think that the baby dinosaurs may have gathered into a group of their own, much the same way modern flamingo hatchlings do. This provided safety in numbers, reducing the risk of being attacked or killed. The adult titanosaurs may have contributed to their safety by patrolling the area around this group of hatchlings. This behavior could have been maintained for weeks until the young titanosaurs were more ready to fend for themselves. Although the scientists do not have any direct evidence for this behavior yet, they believe it is a reasonable explanation of how the young were protected. Otherwise, the babies would have been wiped out easily by marauding theropods, snakes, pterosaurs, and other predatory creatures that lived in the area.

What happened after that is anyone's guess. It seems clear that it would be months—maybe years—before the babies were large enough to keep up with the adult herd. Did they remain in the area or venture out on their own? Nobody knows at this time. One idea is that the young sauropods lived in their own group until they were large enough (juvenile size) to keep up with the adult herd. This seems more than a good guess, because trackways of other sauropod herds have clearly shown that individuals ranging in size from juveniles to adults walked with the herd.[13]

The evidence from Auca Mahuevo suggests that the geographic range and lifestyle of the sauropods were dependent on their size and growth. During the early stages of life, they were small and defenseless and probably stayed near the nesting grounds where they were hatched. During this phase of their life, they were protected by adult sauropods that watched over the nesting grounds.

As they grew larger and able to walk with the largest of their kind, juvenile sauropods probably began to migrate with the herd in its continual search for food. What a remarkable sight it must have been as different generations of these ancient giants traveled together on their journey of survival and discovery.

CHAPTER 4

THE FIRST DISCOVERIES OF DINOSAUR EGGS

When scientists first described dinosaurs in the 1820s, they generally agreed that dinosaurs were some form of reptile. Being reptiles, it was assumed that they probably laid eggs like modern reptiles. But no fossil evidence had been found to support this theory yet. In fact, the chance of finding something as delicate as an egg preserved as a fossil seemed highly unlikely.

Because dinosaur eggs were so fragile, the fact that any of them became fossilized at all is miraculous. Yet some natural forces have preserved fossil evidence of many dinosaur eggs for scientists to examine today. Sudden sandstorms in the Gobi Desert of Mongolia buried dinosaur egg nests.[1] Mud slides and other rapidly occurring natural catastrophes that quickly buried the eggs and nests fossilized nesting sites in other parts of the world, such as in Argentina, France, India, and Montana.

Years later, in 1859, a self-taught naturalist in France named Father Jean-Jacques Pouech found some fossil eggs during one of his frequent hikes in the hills. He wrote an account about them, but he thought they were bird eggs. Ten years later another Frenchman, geologist Phillippe Matheron, discovered large eggshell fragments in the Provence region of southern France. The egg fragments were found with the bones of a large creature that Matheron thought was an extinct crocodile. A colleague of Matheron's, paleontologist Paul Gervais, undertook an extensive study of the eggshell fragments, comparing them to the eggs of other known creatures. Although he couldn't say with certainty that the eggs were from a dinosaur, he suggested that it might be possible. After all, nobody had ever described a dinosaur egg before. It turned out that his guess was a good one because southern France is now known as a rich source of fossil dinosaur eggs.[2]

The discoveries by these French scientists went largely unnoticed in other countries. It wasn't until the 1920s that dinosaur eggs made the headlines in a big way.

A fossil-hunting expedition led by Roy Chapman Andrews of New York's American Museum of Natural History (AMNH) headed for central Asia in search of the origins of man. Andrews led the Central Asiatic Expeditions, a series of well-equipped adventures in 1922, 1923, and 1925. The expeditions did not reveal any evidence of human origins in Asia, but to their great surprise the explorers discovered many dinosaur fossils the likes

In the early 1920s, fossil hunter Roy Chapman Andrews (right) headed to Mongolia. He and his team discovered fossil dinosaurs and dinosaur nests, such as the one shown here.

of which had never before been seen. Two of the dinosaurs discovered were the small *Protoceratops*, an early member of the horned dinosaur family, and *Oviraptor*, a small meat eater. In the same vicinity as these dinosaurs, the team also came across fragments of dinosaur eggs and nests, and skeletons of baby *Protoceratops*. This time, there was no mistaking that the eggs were of dinosaurian origin. It was a spectacular discovery that made news all over the world.

Andrews and his colleagues thought that the eggs belonged to *Protoceratops*, seemingly a safe assumption since so many of those baby dinosaurs had been found near the egg fragments. When they found the remains of a meat eater

A close-up photograph of the dinosaur nest site in Mongolia, 1925.

nearby, they assumed that it was probably gobbling on baby dinosaurs and the eggs of *Protoceratops*. That is why they named the meat eater *Oviraptor*, or "egg thief." However, in 1994, Mark Norell and his colleagues from AMNH revealed that *Oviraptor* had received a bad rap. They found that some of the supposed protoceratopsid eggs contained the remains of *Oviraptor* embryos, making these the first meat-eater eggs positively associated with a specific dinosaur.[3]

The expeditions to Mongolia marked the beginning of widespread scientific interest in fossil dinosaur eggs. Until then, nobody had really been looking for dinosaur eggs. When scientists realized that it was possible for dinosaur eggs to be fossilized, the search was on. Since then, dinosaur eggs have been found on every continent but Antarctica.[4] More than 220 egg sites have been discovered, and three quarters of these are from either North America or Asia.[5]

CHAPTER 5

DINOSAUR EGGS OF MANY SHAPES AND SIZES

One reason that the 1923 Roy Chapman Andrews expedition to Mongolia succeeded in finding dinosaur eggs was that they first noticed a nest that was intact—it actually looked like a nest of eggs. Once they realized what they had found, they were able to look more closely for the remains of other nests and eggs that were less well preserved. Most dinosaur eggs are not found intact: They were usually crushed to smithereens.

What do scientists look for when searching for dinosaur eggs? How can they tell a genuine fossil egg from just a plain old rock? Paleontologists have developed methods and guidelines to help answer these questions. It all begins with an understanding of the purpose and structure of all eggs.

What Is an Egg?

The late Karl F. Hirsch was an expert on eggs, and fossil dinosaur eggs in particular. He described the egg as "the house of an embryo." What he meant by this was that an egg provides everything needed to protect and sustain the life of the baby dinosaur growing inside. The eggshell is like the walls of the house. It protects the embryo by keeping out bacteria and parasites. It is porous so that the embryo can breathe. Fresh air (oxygen) passes in and used air (carbon dioxide) passes out. A nutrient-rich yolk provides food. Water reaches the embryo through the eggshell in the form of water vapor. The embryo also absorbs calcium in the eggshell to help it grow strong bones. Like a house, the egg also maintains a constant temperature and has a place to store body waste.[1]

Fossil dinosaur eggs usually consist of only crushed eggshell. This is what the scientist is most likely to find. Fossil eggshell can be distinguished from other rocks because it has tiny pores and grooves on its outer surface. These are the pores that once allowed air and water vapor to move in and out of the egg.

False Dinosaur Eggs

Many kinds of rock formations can be confused with fossil eggs. Nature happens to make many structures that look so much like eggs that they sometimes fool paleontologists. Some of these look-alikes are concretions, which are made of calcium deposits that form around material in the sediment of a lake or stream. Some are armored mud balls that roll along the bottom of rivers and streams and pick up gravel. Fossilized

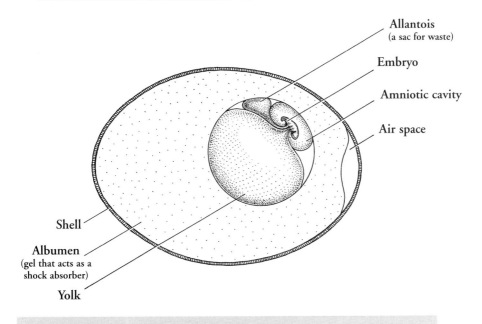

Allantois
(a sac for waste)

Embryo

Amniotic cavity

Air space

Shell

Albumen
(gel that acts as a
shock absorber)

Yolk

The inside of a dinosaur egg

insect burrows may also have an egg shape, as do stomach stones from modern deer, elk, goats, and cattle. These stones form in the stomach to protect the animal when it has swallowed a foreign object. Layers of calcium begin to coat the object in the digestive system, eventually forming a perfect egg shape. The animal then spits it up.[2]

Fake eggs can be detected in several ways. The best clue is the outside surface. A trained eye will detect the pores that make up a true dinosaur eggshell. The outer surface of a concretion, however, consists of grains of sand and does not resemble a porous eggshell. The inside of these objects is also revealing. Most have a sandy, uniform texture because they

These stomach stones were found with the skeleton of *Seismosaurus*. Stomach stones can be confused with dinosaur eggs.

were once merely a ball of mud or sand. They may have layers of deposits in concentric rings that built up over time. Even stomach stones have layers of calcium deposits that a paleontologist would not mistake for the inside of a fossil egg. In addition, a stomach stone contains a hidden treat: the object once swallowed by an animal, which triggered the formation of the stomach stone. In one such case, a stomach stone contained a small lead fishing weight probably swallowed by a deer.[3]

The Classification of Dinosaur Eggs

As with other kinds of fossil discoveries, paleontologists have guidelines for classifying and describing dinosaur eggs. Two basic methods have been tried.

It was first thought that dinosaur eggs should be named after the kind of dinosaur that supposedly laid the eggs. This seemed like a good idea after the discoveries of the famous dinosaurs egg nests in Mongolia in the 1920s. It seemed obvious that these eggs were laid by *Protoceratops*, a dinosaur whose remains were found close to many of the egg remains. But even this case proved troublesome years later when the fossilized embryos of *Oviraptor* were found inside one of these kinds of eggs.[4] It became clear that *Oviraptor* and not *Protoceratops* was responsible for laying at least some of the eggs found in that region of Mongolia. Therefore, it is risky to say that a specific kind of dinosaur laid a particular kind of egg unless a fossilized embryo of that dinosaur is actually found inside one of the eggs. Finding an embryo inside an egg is a rare occurrence. Many thousands of eggs have been found, but few with embryos inside.

Egg classification became further complicated soon after the famous Mongolian discoveries. As paleontologists began to search more closely for fossil dinosaur eggs, it became clear that most new discoveries of dinosaur eggs were without any trace of embryos or other dinosaur bones. Most embryos were probably destroyed soon after the eggs were damaged. In many cases, the heat of the sun probably dried them up, or they were destroyed after being exposed to other natural forces that decayed or eroded them. It is also likely that predators may have eaten a fair share of eggs. Not knowing the occupants of eggs makes naming them after the dinosaur that laid them impossible.

Another way of classifying dinosaur eggs was developed by Chinese paleontologist Zhao Zi-Kui in the 1970s. He relied on an examination of the physical features of the egg and did not worry about which dinosaur may have produced it.[5] In this system, the following basic aspects of a fossil egg are considered:

- size (length, width, volume)
- shape (usually round, oval, or elongate)
- shell thickness
- type of pores in the eggshell
- pattern or ornamentation on the eggshell

Zhao's methods are widely used today. They help to group fossil eggs by similarities in structure. When combined with the infrequent discovery of dinosaur embryos inside eggs, scientists are now better able to associate certain kinds of fossil eggs with particular groups of dinosaurs.

Dinosaur Egg Sizes and Shapes

Fossil dinosaur eggs come in various sizes and shapes, including round, oval, and elongated oval.[6] The smallest known dinosaur eggs are round and only about 3 inches (7.6 centimeters) in diameter. The largest, found in China, are elongate and about 21 inches (54 centimeters) long.

As mentioned earlier, most dinosaur eggs cannot be positively associated with a particular kind of dinosaur. This

This pair of large eggs from China is presumed to have been laid by a meat-eating dinosaur. They measure 18.5 inches long. They were discovered in 1995.

can only be done when the fossilized remains of baby dinosaurs are found in and around fossil eggs. However, Zhao's classification methods combined with existing evidence of dinosaur egg embryos allows paleontologists to make a few assumptions about the eggs of a few different groups of dinosaurs.

Meat Eaters (Theropods). Elongated oval eggs ranging from 5 to 21 inches (13 to 53 centimeters) long, depending on the species of meat eater. These kinds of eggs have been found in Montana, Mongolia, and China. The largest dinosaur eggs currently known were from theropods.

Sauropod eggs recently found in western India were probably laid by titanosaurs. This photo shows a collection of eggs that were excavated from nest sites.

Long-Necked Browsing Plant Eaters (Sauropods). Round eggs, about 5 to 8 inches (13 to 20 centimeters) in diameter, depending on the species of dinosaur. They have been found in many locations, including Spain, Argentina, France, and India. Although the sauropods were the largest known dinosaurs, their eggs were not the largest kinds of dinosaur eggs. Baby sauropods were quite small.

Hadrosaurs (Ornithopod). Round and oval eggs, ranging from about 3 to 8 inches (8 to 20 centimeters) long and 3 to 8 inches (8 to 20 centimeters) wide.[7] The duck-billed dinosaur *Maiasaura* from Montana is now famous because of the discoveries of paleontologist Jack Horner at Egg Mountain in northwestern Montana. Although Horner and his colleagues have found an abundance of baby dinosaurs, nests, and eggshell, the actual shape of these eggs is not positively known. These eggs have been found only in tiny fragments.

However, remains of hadrosaurs and associated eggs in Mongolia and Alberta confirm a rounded oval shape for duck-billed dinosaur eggs.[8] Hadrosaur eggs from Devil's Coulee, Alberta, Canada, are among the largest eggs known for any dinosaur. They are round, almost the size of soccer balls, and have a recorded volume of 3.8 liters for eggs that were about 8 inches (20 centimeters) in diameter.

Armored, Plated, and Bone-Headed Dinosaurs. There are no reports of fossil eggs for armored, plated, or bone-headed dinosaurs. Being ornithischians, it is possible that their eggs were similar to those of distantly related horned or ornithopod dinosaurs. Dinosaur egg expert Kenneth Carpenter speculates that their eggs were probably round and about the size of a navel orange or grapefruit. But he and other scientists admit that they really do not know enough to make an accurate guess about the eggs of these dinosaurs. Finding eggs of the armored and plated dinosaurs is made even more challenging because many lived so much longer ago—in the

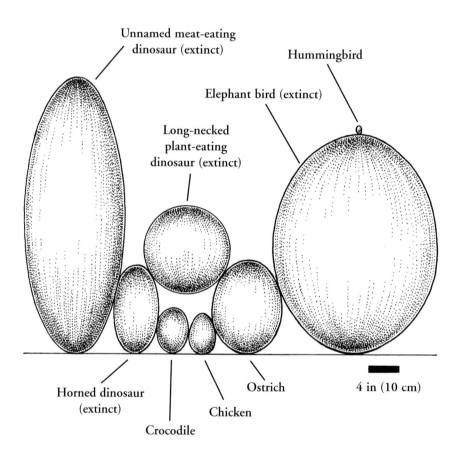

Unnamed meat-eating
dinosaur (extinct)

Hummingbird

Elephant bird (extinct)

Long-necked
plant-eating
dinosaur (extinct)

Horned dinosaur
(extinct)

Crocodile

Chicken

Ostrich

4 in (10 cm)

Eggs sizes can vary, as shown here by the eggs of dinosaurs, birds, and a crocodile.

Jurassic Period—than those dinosaurs for whom eggs are most frequently found.

Horned Dinosaurs. Horned dinosaurs had elliptical eggs with one end more pointed than the other. The eggs were about 4.4 inches long by 2.5 inches wide (11 centimeters long by 6 centimeters wide). Although the discovery of embryos within such eggs has not been confirmed, elliptical eggs of this type have been found in deposits containing the bones of *Protoceratops, Centrosaurus, Chasmosaurus,* and *Psittacosaurus.* The size of a probable *Protoceratops* egg clutch is about eighteen eggs laid in concentric circles.

These egg sizes may seem quite small for creatures that would soon grow to be many thousands of times larger than their egg. Imagine a newly hatched long-necked browsing dinosaur. Specimens recently discovered in Argentina began life at a mere 15 inches (38 centimeters) long. They would grow to become adults that were 45 feet (13.7 meters) long and weighed many tons. Their eggs were round and small, only about 6 inches (15 centimeters) in diameter.[9] One of the secrets of the success of the dinosaurs was that they had an active metabolism and grew rapidly. Therefore, even the largest creatures ever to walk the earth were able to begin life in the compact protective shell of a relatively small egg. This made it possible for the mother to have more offspring to more easily further the survival of the species.

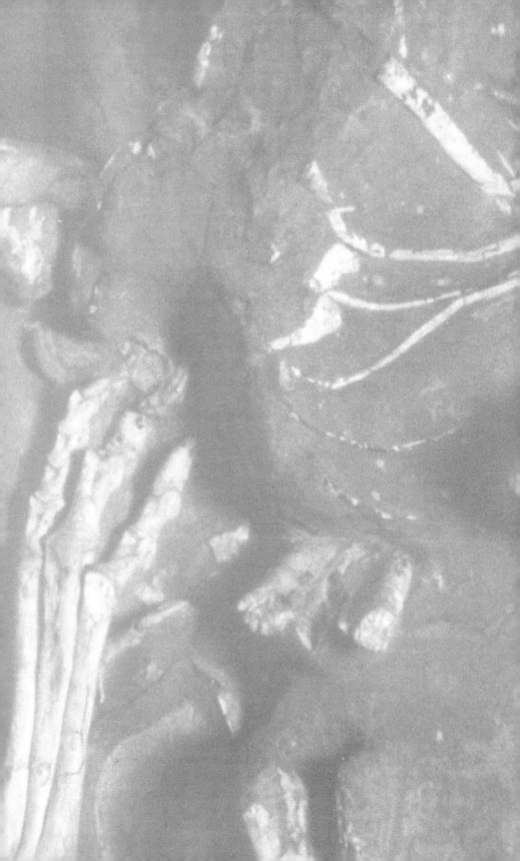

CHAPTER 6

DINOSAUR NESTS

Dinosaurs laid their eggs in nests on the ground. No one is sure what these nests actually looked like, though. Did dinosaurs cover their eggs with mud and vegetation? Were the eggs exposed to the warm sun? There are clues that point to these and other possibilities. Just like birds today, different kinds of dinosaurs probably behaved in different ways when it came to building nests. One thing we know for sure is that dinosaurs had many different kinds of nesting habits.

Evidence about dinosaur nests comes mainly from looking at the arrangement of fossilized eggs that were laid together as a group. Sometimes the outline of a nest is preserved in the form of a shallow earthen pit into which the eggs were laid. The duck-billed *Maiasaura* laid its eggs inside a bowl-like pit that the dinosaur formed from a mound of surrounding mud.[1]

Nesting Patterns

Dinosaur nests did not all look alike. One important reason for this is that the biggest dinosaurs simply needed more room to lay their eggs than smaller dinosaurs. The size of the mother dinosaur greatly influenced the design of the nest. The size, shape, and number of eggs she would lay also affected the design of the nest.

Dinosaurs laid their eggs in one of two basic clutch patterns: groups of eggs laid in a cluster and eggs laid in rows.[2]

Nests of Meat-Eating Dinosaurs. The small Mongolian theropod *Oviraptor* laid its elongate eggs in a ring within a shallow nesting pit that it probably dug from the dirt and sand. These nests usually contained up to twenty-four eggs arranged in a circle. The eggs rested slightly upright. The ring pattern is similar to that seen in brooding birds such as chickens, which sit on their nest to keep the eggs warm. Occasionally, when a large number of eggs of this type are found, they are arranged as concentric circles—a ring within a ring. A nest of *Troodon* found in Montana consisted of twenty-four eggs arranged in this manner. The most eggs found in a nest were of this type. It included forty eggs that

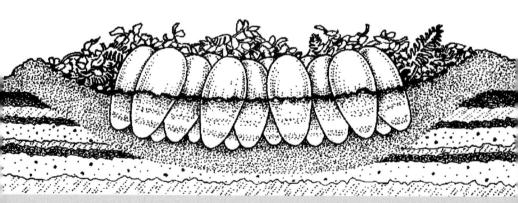

A nest of *Troodon* eggs shows that theropods laid their eggs with the narrow end pointing down in to the ground.

troodontid
hatchling

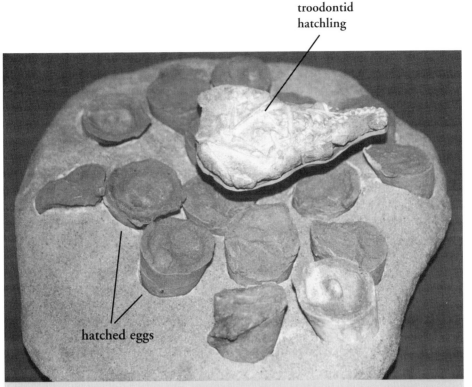

hatched eggs

This nest of a small troodontid meat eater was discovered in Mongolia. It includes the remains of hatched eggs and the skeleton of a hatchling resting on top.

had been layered in tiers.[3] Other small meat-eating dinosaurs probably used a ring strategy like *Oviraptor* or *Troodon*.

The largest eggs found near any dinosaurs are thought to be from meat eaters. They were elongate and a whopping 21 inches (53.3 centimeters) long. In at least one case, a nest of these giant eggs consisted of about twenty-six eggs laid in pairs in a large ring about 7 feet (2.1 meters) across.

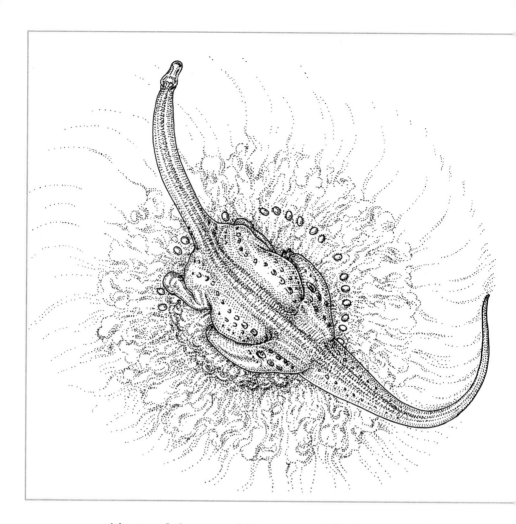

Nests of Sauropod Dinosaurs. The large round eggs associated with sauropod dinosaurs were about 6 to 12 inches (15 to 30 centimeters) long. They have been found in many places around the world. Clutches of these eggs generally have about twelve closely packed eggs laid in a single layer, although cases with as few as three and as many as twenty eggs have also been found.

Sauropod eggs and nests are best represented by a group of sauropods called the titanosaurs. Titanosaurs were widespread during the Cretaceous Period. Their remains have been found

Some sauropods may have been too big to lay all of their eggs in one small pit. Instead, they may have laid their egg clutches in a wide arc, giving them more room to maneuver their large bodies (left). The picture above shows the posture of a female titanosaur while she is laying her eggs.

in Spain, France, India, Argentina, and other countries. These same locations are also known for numerous dinosaur egg nests that were probably created by titanosaurs. They offer our best clues about the nesting habits of sauropods. These nests were made in two common patterns, most likely used by sauropods of different sizes:[4]

- Six to twelve eggs laid in a circular pit that may have been dug out by the forelimbs of the sauropod. The large inside claws on the front legs of sauropods may have been great tools for making these pits. These nest patterns have been found in Spain and Argentina.

This clutch of fossil eggs was laid by a small meat eater. It was discovered in China in 1995.

- Fifteen to twenty eggs laid in semicircular arcs instead of tight clutches. It appears that this type of pattern, observed in France, may have matched the turning motion of the squatting female as she laid her eggs. This would have helped her avoid accidentally stomping on her eggs after depositing them.

A third nest pattern is also tentatively attributed to sauropods. Eggs laid in linear pairs found in France are thought to be those of a sauropod.

Sauropod and hadrosaur nesting grounds sometimes contain nests that have been stacked on top of other nests.

This evidence suggests that dinosaurs returned to the same nesting grounds every season. They created new nests on top of the remains of old ones.[5]

Nests of Duck-Billed Dinosaurs. Nests associated with the remains of hadrosaurs have been discovered in Montana, China, Mongolia, and Kyrgyzstan. The eggs of duck-billed dinosaurs were oval and smaller than the rounded eggs of sauropods. Measuring up to 5 inches (12.7 centimeters) long and 4.7 inches (12 centimeters) wide, these eggs were usually

The circular shape of fossil sauropod eggs can clearly be seen in this partial nest discovered in western India.

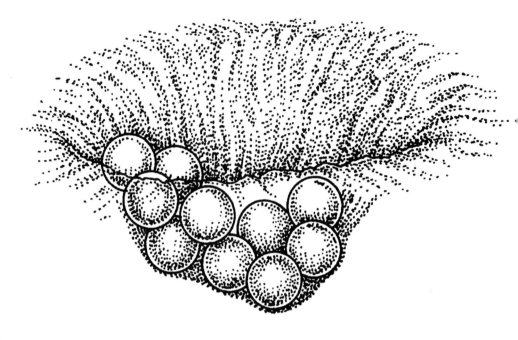

Some sauropods laid six to twelve eggs in a circular pit that may have been dug out by the forelimbs of the mother.

laid in one or two layers in a shallow pit. As many as thirty-four of these eggs have been discovered in a single nest.[6]

Many nests of the hadrosaur *Maiasaura* have been found in northwestern Montana. A typical example consists of a shallow pit about 6.5 feet (2 meters) across. The nests are separated by a distance of about 24 feet (7.3 meters), which is about the length of an adult *Maiasaura*. This suggests that the nests were part of a colony of nests that was occupied by many *Maiasaura* at the same time, probably by a migrating herd. Each mother dinosaur would have had enough room to create her nest and lay her eggs without disturbing her neighbor. *Maiasaura* nests have an organized clutch pattern consisting of one or two layers of eggs arranged in a circle. Nests have been found with fourteen to eighteen eggs in them.[7]

Another example of a possible hadrosaur nest has a different nesting pattern than that of *Maiasaura*. The nest was discovered in Romania and consists of two layers of eggs laid in linear rows, one atop the other. There were three or four eggs per row.[8]

Protection and Incubation of Eggs

Like eggs with which we are familiar today, dinosaur eggs required a period of incubation. The embryo inside needs time to develop into an individual strong enough to hatch into the

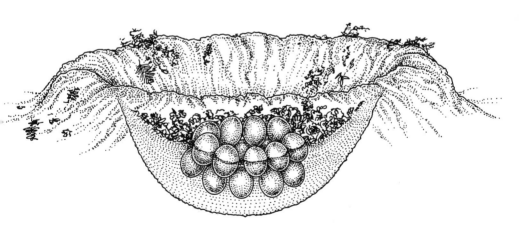

Maiasaura nests have one or two layers of eggs arranged in a circle.

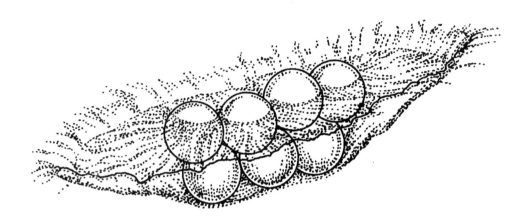

This hadrosaur nest in Romania had two layers of eggs laid in rows, one atop the other.

outside world. A nest provides protection for eggs during the incubation period.

The two basic ways to incubate eggs are by burying them or sitting on them to keep them warm with body heat (brooding). Did dinosaurs use either of these techniques? The arrangement of eggs within the nests provides clues about how the eggs were incubated.

Scientists assume that the largest kinds of dinosaurs were simply too big to brood a nest of eggs. Adults probably had to keep a safe distance from the eggs once they had been laid to avoid crushing them underfoot. These dinosaurs probably protected and incubated their nests by covering the eggs with mud or vegetation. This is typical of the round eggs associated

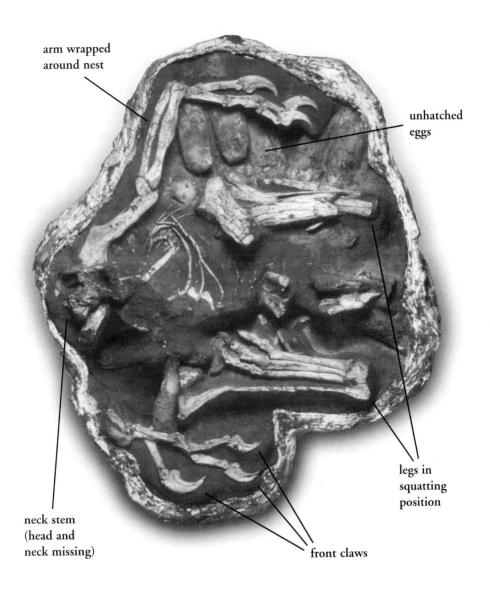

arm wrapped
around nest

unhatched
eggs

legs in
squatting
position

neck stem
(head and
neck missing)

front claws

This fossil nest discovered in Mongolia shows clear evidence that some small meat eaters protected their nests. The dinosaur is *Oviraptor*.

with sauropod dinosaurs. These eggs were often laid in a small pit and were probably held in place by mud or sand mounded on top. They were often piled together in no particular pattern, often in several layers. A partial covering of mud would have retained heat from the sun and kept the eggs warm, even into the night.

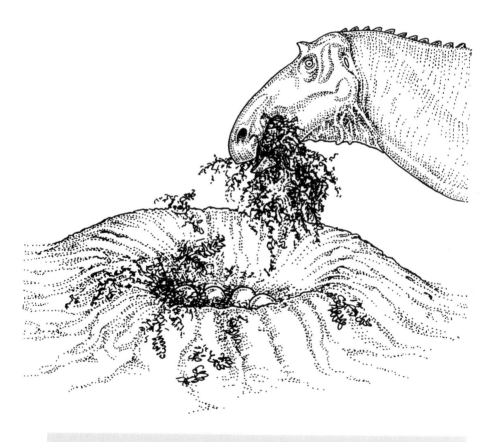

Some dinosaurs, such as hadrosaurs, probably covered their nests with vegetation to protect the eggs and keep them warm. This would help the eggs incubate.

Some dinosaur nests show a more orderly arrangement of the eggs, such as a circle. In one case, this kind of nest was found with the skeleton of an adult dinosaur sitting in the middle of a ring of eggs. The dinosaur in question was the small meat eater *Oviraptor*, found in Mongolia. This evidence strongly suggests that the dinosaur was brooding its nest of eggs.[9] However, paleontologist Kenneth Carpenter disagrees with this interpretation. He believes that the ring of eggs in the case of the nesting *Oviraptor* was too wide for the dinosaur to have actually been sitting on them. Instead, he suggests that the adult *Oviraptor* was probably positioned inside the nest to protect its clutch.[10] Brooding—or protecting—eggs in this manner may have been common among small meat-eating dinosaurs whose nests had a clutch pattern of an oval or ring. The circular pattern would have been important so that the adult dinosaur could sit in the middle without crushing the eggs.

CHAPTER 7

WHOSE EGGS WERE THEY ANYWAY?

One of the first questions anyone has about a dinosaur egg is, what dinosaur made it? The only way to tell for sure whether an egg belongs to a certain kind of dinosaur is to find identifiable bones inside an unhatched fossil egg. These would be the remains of an embryo—a dinosaur that had been growing inside the egg. Fossil dinosaur embryos are not discovered often, but when they are, the evidence can be spectacular.

The chances of finding a fossil embryo are poor. Even though many dinosaur eggs have been discovered, only a fraction of a percentage have remains of embryos inside. This is largely due to the delicate nature of an embryo itself. Unless it died at a late stage of development—after its bones had largely formed—there wouldn't have been much to become fossilized. Most dinosaur eggs show little inside except the sediment that seeped into the egg cavity when the eggs were becoming fossilized. Any soft parts, such as the yolk or skin and organs of the embryo, would have decayed and been lost forever.

Peeking Inside an Egg

Do paleontologists break open fossil eggs to look for embryos? Not in most cases. Because many fossil dinosaur eggs are discovered in a fragmented or broken state, paleontologists can often peek inside the egg because it is already broken. Once an egg is open or in pieces, they can pick apart the inside of the egg to search for embryonic bones. Unbroken fossil eggs are rare treasures. Breaking one open to study its contents is normally an unacceptable risk, unless the paleontologist has a clue that what hides inside will be more valuable once it is exposed.

There is a way to look inside an egg without damaging it. The medical technology of computed tomography, or CT scanning, is used to create electronic images of the inside of a body. This same technology can be used to scan the inside of fossil dinosaur eggs, but with mixed results.

CT scanning electronically records thin sections of the inside of a specimen. Using a computer, the multiple slices are assembled into a three-dimensional image. The result is a view of the inside of the specimen made up of multiple sections. CT scanning is more effective than X rays because it records finer details and presents them in three dimensions. This allows the scientist to pinpoint the location of any possible remains seen in an egg.

CT scanning is not foolproof. It can easily mislead people who have had little experience examining fossil dinosaur eggs. According to dinosaur egg specialist Kenneth Carpenter, what you see in a CT scan of a dinosaur egg isn't always what you get. Ken explains that in the dinosaur eggs he has studied, "The embryo settles to the bottom of the egg, where it decays, leaving a layer of bone against the shell."[1] This may or may not represent embryonic material. Ken has never seen a fossil embryo suspended by rock in the middle of an egg. He says that the sediment filling a fossil egg varies widely in density and can be confused with fossil remains. He suspects that the "floating" embryos seen in some CT scans are patches of rock of different densities. He has never seen embryonic bone appear in a CT scan because it is the same hardness as the rock and blends in.

Investigating the insides of a dinosaur egg is still a relatively new branch of paleontology. If a CT scan suggests that something spectacular might be hidden inside, a paleontologist can use this information to decide if it is worthwhile to crack the egg and examine the material more closely.

Known Dinosaur Embryos

Some remarkable discoveries in recent years have greatly increased scientists' knowledge of which dinosaurs laid which kinds of eggs. Although the bones of unhatched dinosaurs are delicate and small, some identifying features such as the shape of the skull allow scientists to clearly identify which dinosaur is inside an egg.

As mentioned earlier, there is a form of large, round dinosaur egg frequently found in nests in Europe, India, and Argentina. Paleontologists have long thought that these eggs were those of sauropods because the bones of adult and juvenile sauropods had been found in the same general area. However, scientists are eager to avoid yet another case of mistaken identity like that of *Protoceratops* and *Oviraptor*. They have been waiting for embryonic remains found within an egg itself to provide supporting evidence for this assumption. A spectacular discovery in South America has now put this debate to rest.

The first indisputable evidence that sauropods laid round eggs came in late 1998 from the desolate badlands of Argentina known as Patagonia. A fossil-hunting team led by Luis Chiappe, then of the American Museum of Natural History, had come across the discovery of a lifetime. It was a vast expanse of fossils, spreading for more than a square mile. Much of the area was a huge dinosaur nesting site, one of the largest ever discovered. But something had gone terribly wrong there about 80 million years ago. A natural disaster, most likely a flood, washed out the area and buried thousands of dinosaur nests in mud.[2]

The site was given the clever name of Auca Mahuevo, combining a reference to an extinct volcano in the area named Auca Mahuida with the Spanish words *más huevos*, meaning "more eggs." The dinosaurs that once frequented the area were titanosaurs. These sauropods from the Southern Hemisphere have also been found throughout Africa, Europe, and India,

This is most likely a nest of titanosaurs. It was discovered in northwestern Patagonia, Argentina.

all of which were connected at one time by land bridges. To the delight of the team, many of the intact eggs and partial eggs contained fossilized fragments of embryonic titanosaur skeletons. This evidence of baby titanosaurs before they had hatched clinched the theory that such round eggs were those of sauropod dinosaurs.[3] The team even recovered fossil skin casts, the first for any variety of embryonic dinosaur specimen. They clearly show the reptilian scales that made up its skin. The embryonic titanosaurs measured about 12 inches (30 centimeters) long inside the egg.[4]

The Patagonian egg site is so extensive that Argentine paleontologist Rodolfo Coria believes it will take many years to fully explore. He calls the site "unique," a once-in-a-lifetime opportunity to study the entire ecosystem of these dinosaurs. The area not only includes fossils of the titanosaurs and their eggs, but of ancient plant life and other creatures, perhaps even other dinosaurs, that lived in the same area.[5]

The titanosaur embryos from Patagonia join only a small group of embryonic remains known for any dinosaurs. The rarity of fossil embryo discoveries is remarkable. Given the thousands of fossil dinosaur eggs that have been found, only about twenty-one are currently known to have included embryonic dinosaur remains that were complete enough to identify the parent (see Table 2).

Large Dinosaurs From Tiny Eggs

When you think about dinosaurs from now on, remember that even the largest of them began life as small, often helpless

Table 2. Known Dinosaur Fossil Embryos[6]

Dinosaur	Location and Date Described	Period
Sauropods		
Camarasaurus	Colorado, 1994	Late Jurassic
*Mussaurus**	Argentina, 1979	Late Triassic
titanosaur (unnamed)	Argentina, 1998	Late Cretaceous
Theropods		
Oviraptor	Mongolia, 1994	Late Cretaceous
giant oviraptorid (unnamed)	China, 1995	Late Cretaceous
Scipionyx	Italy, 1998	Early Cretaceous
segnosaur (unnamed)	China, 1995	Late Cretaceous
theropod (two specimens, unnamed)	Portugal, 1997	Late Jurassic
Troodon	Montana, 1996	Late Cretaceous
Troodon	Wyoming, 1982	Late Cretaceous
Velociraptor	Mongolia, 1994	Late Cretaceous
Ornithopods		
Camptosaurus	Utah, 1994	Late Jurassic
Dryosaurus	Colorado, 1991	Late Jurassic
hadrosaur (unnamed)	Mongolia, 1983	Late Cretaceous
Hypacrosaurus	Alberta, 1994	Late Cretaceous
hypsilophodont (unnamed)	Texas, 1989	Early Cretaceous
Maiasaura	Montana, 1988	Late Cretaceous
Ceratopsia		
Bagaceratops	Mongolia, 1975	Late Cretaceous
Protoceratops	Mongolia, 1975	Late Cretaceous
Psittacosaurus	Mongolia, 1982	Early Cretaceous

*Could possibly be hatchlings and not embryos

This is the embryo of a titanosaur as it would have been positioned in its egg.

babies. As reptiles go, dinosaurs were highly unusual in that some kinds seem to have taken great care of their young. This behavior, not seen to this extent in living reptiles, gives the dinosaurs traits that remind us more of mammals and birds.

The search for dinosaur eggs and babies is one of the great new frontiers in dinosaur science. Scientists now look closely underfoot to find evidence of nests, eggs, and dinosaur young. If you would like to work in the world of paleontology one day, the study of dinosaur eggs and babies would be a great place to start.

Chapter Notes

Chapter 2. Dinosaur Hatchlings and Babies

1. Kenneth Carpenter, Karl F. Hirsch, and John R. Horner, eds., *Dinosaur Eggs and Babies* (New York: Cambridge University Press, 1994), p. 256.

2. Luis M. Chiappe, Rodolfo A. Coria, Lowell L. Dingus, F. Jackson, Anusaya Chinsamy, and M. Fox, "Sauropod Dinosaur Embryos from the Late Cretaceous of Patagonia," *Nature*, no. 396, 1998, pp. 258–261.

3. Personal communication with Kenneth Carpenter, August 11, 2000.

Chapter 3. Family Life

1. John R. Horner and James Gorman, *Digging Dinosaurs* (New York: Workman, 1988), p. 108.

2. Kenneth Carpenter, Karl F. Hirsch, and John R. Horner, eds., *Dinosaur Eggs and Babies* (New York: Cambridge University Press, 1994), p. 42.

3. Ibid., p. 235.

4. David E. Fastovsky and David B. Weishampel, *The Evolution and Extinction of the Dinosaurs* (Cambridge, England: Cambridge University Press, 1996), p. 221.

5. Carpenter, Hirsch, and Horner, p. 322.

6. Luis M. Chiappe and Lowell Dingus, *Walking on Eggs* (New York: Scribner, 2001), p. 173.

7. Horner and Gorman, p. 104.

8. Ibid., p. 128.

9. Ibid., p. 104.

10. David B. Weishampel, David E. Fastovsky, M. Watabe, R. Barsbold, and Kh. Tsogtbaatar, "New Embryonic and Hatchling Dinosaur Remains from the Late Cretaceous of Mongolia," *Journal of Vertebrate Paleontology Abstracts of Papers*, vol. 20, supplement to no. 3, September 25, 2000, p. 78A.

11. Chiappe and Dingus, p. 171.

12. Ibid., p. 180.

13. Martin Lockley and Adrian P. Hunt, *Dinosaur Tracks* (New York: Columbia University Press, 1995), pp. 164–173.

Chapter 4. The First Discoveries of Dinosaur Eggs

1. Zhiming Dong and Philip J. Currie, "On the Discovery of an Oviraptorid Skeleton on a Nest of Eggs at Bayan Mandahu, Inner Mongolia, People's Republic of China," *Canadian Journal of Earth Science*, vol. 33, 1996, pp. 631–636.

2. Kenneth Carpenter, *Eggs, Nests, and Baby Dinosaurs* (Bloomington, Ind.: Indiana University Press, 1999), pp. 6–7.

3. Mark A. Norell, J. M. Clark, D. Demberelyin, B. Rinchen, Luis M. Chiappe, A. R. Davidson, M. C. McKenna, P. Altangerel, and Michael J. Novacek, "A Theropod Dinosaur Embryo and the Affinities of the Flaming Cliffs Dinosaur Eggs," *Science*, vol. 266, pp. 779–782.

4. Luis M. Chiappe and Lowell Dingus, *Walking on Eggs* (New York: Scribner, 2001), p. 79.

5. Kenneth Carpenter, Karl F. Hirsch, and John R. Horner, eds., *Dinosaur Eggs and Babies* (New York: Cambridge University Press, 1994), pp. 15–30.

Chapter 5. Dinosaur Eggs of Many Shapes and Sizes

1. James O. Farlow and Michael K. Brett-Surman, eds., *The Complete Dinosaur* (Bloomington, Ind.: Indiana University Press, 1997), pp. 394–396.

2. Kenneth Carpenter, *Eggs, Nests, and Baby Dinosaurs* (Bloomington, Ind.: Indiana University Press, 1999), pp. 120–121.

3. Ibid.

4. Mark A. Norell, J. M. Clark, D. Demberelyin, B. Rinchen, Luis M. Chiappe, A. R. Davidson, M. C. McKenna, P. Altangerel, and Michael J. Novacek, "A Theropod Dinosaur Embryo and the Affinities of the Flaming Cliffs Dinosaur Eggs," *Science*, vol. 266, pp. 779–782.

5. Ibid., pp. 148–150.

6. Kenneth Carpenter, Karl F. Hirsch, and John R. Horner, eds., *Dinosaur Eggs and Babies* (New York: Cambridge University Press, 1994), p. 1.

7. Karl F. Hirsch and B. Quinn, "Eggs and Eggshell Fragments from the Upper Cretaceous Two Medicine Formation of Montana," *Journal of Vertebrate Paleontology*, vol. 10, no. 4, 1990, pp. 491–511.

8. Carpenter, p. 210.

9. Luis M. Chiappe, Rodolfo A. Coria, Lowell L. Dingus, F. Jackson, Anusaya Chinsamy, and M. Fox, "Sauropod Dinosaur Embryos from the Late Cretaceous of Patagonia," *Nature*, no. 396, 1998, pp. 258–261.

Chapter 6. Dinosaur Nests

1. John R. Horner and Robert Makela, "Nest of Juveniles Provides Evidence of Family Structure Among Dinosaurs," Nature, vol. 82, 1979, pp. 296–298.

2. Kenneth Carpenter, Karl F. Hirsch, and John R. Horner, eds., *Dinosaur Eggs and Babies* (New York: Cambridge University Press, 1994), p. 37.

3. Kenneth Carpenter, *Eggs, Nests, and Baby Dinosaurs* (Bloomington, Ind.: Indiana University Press, 1999), p. 171.

4. Carpenter, Hirsch, and Horner, p. 37.

5. Ibid., p. 41.

6. Carpenter, p. 282.

7. John R. Horner and James Gorman, *Digging Dinosaurs* (New York: Workman, 1988), p. 107.

8. Carpenter, Hirsch, and Horner, p. 77.

9. Mark Norell, James Clark, Luis Chiappe, and D. Dashzeveg, "A Nesting Dinosaur," *Nature*, vol. 378, 1995, pp. 774–776.

10. Carpenter, p. 156.

Chapter 7. Whose Eggs Were They Anyway?

1. Personal communication with Kenneth Carpenter, August 11, 2000.

2. Luis M.Chiappe, "Dinosaur Embryos," *National Geographic*, December 1998, pp. 34–41.

3. Luis M. Chiappe, Rodolfo A. Coria, Lowell L. Dingus, F. Jackson, Anusaya Chinsamy, and M. Fox, "Sauropod Dinosaur Embryos from the Late Cretaceous of Patagonia," *Nature*, no. 396, 1998, pp. 258–261.

4. Luis M. Chiappe and Lowell Dingus, *Walking on Eggs* (New York: Scribner, 2001), p. 173.

5. Personal communication with Rodolfo Coria, April 1999.

6. Adapted from Kenneth Carpenter, *Eggs, Nests, and Baby Dinosaurs* (Bloomington, Ind.: Indiana University Press, 1999), p. 203.

GLOSSARY

ankylosaur—Any of the armored dinosaurs.

carnivore—A meat-eating creature.

Ceratopsia—"Horned face." The order of horned dinosaurs, including the psittacosaurs, protoceratopsids, and ceratopsids.

clutch—A group of eggs in a nest.

concentric—Arranged with their centers overlapping.

Cretaceous Period—The third and final major time division (144 to 65 million years ago) of the Mesozoic Era. The end of the age of dinosaurs.

eggshell—The hard protective outer layer of an egg, composed primarily of calcium carbonate.

embryo—A vertebrate organism before it hatches or is born.

evolution—The patterns of change through time of living organisms.

extinction—The irreversible elimination of an entire species of plant or animal.

herbivore—A plant-eating creature.

Jurassic Period—The second of the three major time divisions (208 to 144 million years ago) of the Mesozoic Era.

Mesozoic Era—The time of the dinosaurs (245 to 65 million years ago).

nest—A structure made by a bird, reptile, or dinosaur for the protection and incubation of its eggs. Nests may be located on the ground, in the ground, or in a tree or other elevated spot.

Ornithischia—One of two groups of dinosaurs based on hip structure. Ornithischians had a hip with a backward-pointing pubis bone.

ornithopods—A group of two-footed ornithischian, plant-eating dinosaurs.

paleontologist—A scientist who studies life-forms of the geologic past, especially through the analysis of plant and animal fossils.

predator—A meat-eating creature.

protoceratopsids—"First horned face." A subfamily of the Ceratopsians including small frilled dinosaurs lacking nose and brow horns. Includes *Protoceratops*.

psittacosaurs—"Parrot lizards." A subfamily of the Ceratopsians representing the earliest members of this group. Includes *Psittacosaurus*.

Saurischia—One of two groups of dinosaurs based on hip structure. Saurischians had a hip with a forward-pointing pubis bone.

sauropod—Large plant-eating saurischian dinosaurs with long necks and long tails.

stegosaur—Any of the plated dinosaurs.

theropod—Any of a group of saurischian dinosaurs that ate meat and walked on two legs.

trackway—Fossilized footprints.

Triassic Period—The first of the three major time divisions (245 to 208 million years ago) of the Mesozoic Era.

vertebra—A bone of the neck, spine, or tail.

vertebrate—Any animal that has a backbone (spine).

yolk—A nutrient-rich sac inside an egg that is an embryo's main source of food.

FURTHER READING

Even though there have been hundreds of books about dinosaurs published, reputable dinosaur books are hard to find. Listed here are some of the authors' favorites on the subject of dinosaur eggs, nests, and babies.

Books

Bakker, Robert T. *The Dinosaur Heresies.* New York: William Morrow and Company, 1986.

Carpenter, Kenneth. *Eggs, Nests, and Baby Dinosaurs.* Bloomington, Ind.: Indiana University Press, 1999.

Carpenter, Kenneth, Karl F. Hirsch, and John R. Horner. *Dinosaur Eggs and Babies.* New York: Cambridge University Press, 1994.

Chiappe, Luis M., and Lowell Dingus. *Walking on Eggs.* New York: Scribner, 2001.

Colbert, Edwin H. *The Great Dinosaur Hunters and Their Discoveries.* New York: Dover Publications, 1984.

Farlow, James O., and Michael K. Brett-Surman (eds.). *The Complete Dinosaur.* Bloomington, Ind.: Indiana University Press, 1997.

Horner, John R., and James Gorman. *Digging Dinosaurs.* New York: Workman, 1988.

INTERNET ADDRESSES

American Museum of Natural History. *Fossil Halls*, n.d. <http://www.amnh.org/exhibitions/Fossil_Halls/?src=i_ph>.

Denver Museum of Natural History. *Research: Cedar Mountain Dinosaur Project*. n.d. <http://www.dmnh.org/cedarmnt/cmnt_17.htm>.

Jacobson, Russ. *Dino Russ's Lair: Dinosaur and Vertebrate Paleontology Information*. n.d. <http://www.isgs.uiuc.edu/dinos/dinos_home.html>.

National Geographic Society. *Dinosaur Eggs*. n.d. <www.nationalgeographic.com/dinoeggs/>.

Natural History Museum of Los Angeles County. *Project Patagonia*. n.d. <http://www.nhm.org/projectpatagonia/home.html>.

Summer, Edward. *The Dinosaur Interplanetary Gazette*. n.d. <http://www.dinosaur.org/frontpage.html>.

University of Bristol. *Dinobase*. n.d. <http://palaeo.gly.bris.ac.uk/dinobase/dinopage.html>.

University of California Museum of Paleontology, Berkeley, and the Regents of the University of California. *The Dinosauria: Truth Is Stranger Than Fiction*. © 1994–2002. <www.ucmp.berkeley.edu/diapsids/dinosaur.html>.

INDEX